BETWEEN THE HOUSES

Margot Fortunato Galt

with art by Delor Erickson

LAUREL
POETRY
COLLECTIVE

Particular thanks to those who helped with this book:
Jill Breckenridge, Robert Hedin, Ann Iverson, Deborah Keenan,
Monica Ochtrup, Sylvia Ruud

ACKNOWLEDGMENTS

"Southern Combustion" previously appeared in *Begin with a Blank Page* (Norcroft: A Writing Retreat for Women, Tenth Anniversary Anthology, 1993–2003); "Her Letter to a Patron" and "Walking by the Wall" in *Border Crossings* (New Rivers Press, 1984); "Relations," "Grandmother," and "Painted Cheeks" in *The Country's Way with Rain*, limited edition chapbook by Margot Fortunato Galt (Kutenai Press, 1994); "The White Room" in *Poems* (The Billie Murray Denny Award poems, 1991–1992); "Missionary" in *Great River Review*; "Florence Nightingale Receives a Visitor" in *The Iowa Review*; "Bridge of Sighs" in *Italian Americana*; "The Scarf" in *The Louisville Review*; "My Mother's Leaving" in *Looking for Home: Women Writing about Exile* (Milkweed Editions, 1990); "At the Edge Together" in *Loonfeather*; "Midwestern Epic" in *Milkweed Chronicle*; "Uncle Tonio" in *Mr. Cogito*; "The Annunciation" in *The Poet Dreaming in the Artist's House: Contemporary Poems about the Visual Arts* (Milkweed Editions, 1984) and *Great River Review*; "Late Song" in *Pulling for Good News* (Laurel Poetry Collective, 2004); "The Last Seal," "The Iris Garden," "Translate," and "Galleries" in *Sing Heavenly Muse!*; "After Dachau" in *Spoon River Poetry Review*; "The Chicken," "Evening Drive: Consolation," and "Dakota Turkey" in *Water~Stone*; "Chokecherry Summers" in *Woman Poet: Midwest*.

© 2004 Margot Fortunato Galt

Art © 2004 Delor Erickson

All rights reserved.

Printed in the United States of America.

Published by LAUREL POETRY COLLECTIVE
1168 Laurel Avenue, St. Paul MN 55104
www.laurelpoetry.com

Book design by Sylvia Ruud

Library of Congress Cataloging-in-Publication Data
Galt, Margot Fortunato.
    Between the houses / by Margot Fortunato Galt.
       p. cm.
    ISBN 0-9728934-9-0
    I. Title.
PS3607.A425B48 2004
811'.6—dc22

                       2004015836

CONTENTS

Between the Houses: It Must Be Morning   7
    The Egg   8
    The Annunciation   9
    At the Edge Together   10
    Midwestern Epic   11
    Chokecherry Summers   12
    Dakota Turkey   14
    Uncle Tonio   15

Between the Houses: Old Notions   19
    Relations   20
    To My Mother at 82   21
    Painted Cheeks   22
    Grandmother   23
    Math Whiz   24
    Missionary   25

Between the Houses: Soot   27
    Orion's Sword   28
    Winter Mood   30
    Body Count   31
    Bridge of Sighs   32

Between the Houses: Glacial Eyebrows   35
    Gravestones   36
    Walking by the Wall   37
    The Iris Garden   38
    Galleries   40
    The Chicken   41
    The Last Seal in the Baltic   42

Between the Houses: Summer Sideshow   45
    My Mother's Leaving   46
    Mudpies   48
    Southern Combustion 1959   49
    Her Letter to a Patron   51
    Florence Nightingale Receives a Visitor   53

Between the Houses: March Thaw   55
    After Dachau   56
    The White Room   59
    To the Funeral and After   61
    Late Song   63

Between the Houses: Glad Hand   65
    Translate   66
    The Scarf   68
    Evening Drive: Consolation   70
    No More Back of the Bus   72
    The Ground Carries Us   74
    Cellini's Forge   75
    Walking the Labyrinth at Villa Maria   76

Between the Houses:

It Must Be Morning

Sun squares yellow
on the back
of a distant house.

After weeks of
covering your eyes,
you have to admit
when this moment falls—
roof, walls shimmer
with a passion that
will not let you in.

You can blame the charm
of lives inside,
chalk it up
to a trick of light.

But if you watch long enough
you'll see how the old
architecture of desire—

parabola of bay,
elbow of eaves—

has taken hold.
Then, conquest assured,

it rebuttons its plackets
and ruches

in the heavy sun.

The Egg

Mrs. Green steps out in a flowery dress.
Her high heels sink in mud.

White chicken navigates better.
She raises her wings.
Spring stirs her warm fowl blood.

Does she care for the rooster
with wobbly comb, stuffed shirtfront?
Is she concerned for
this bureaucrat of the mating season?

The white chicken scratches.
Impulse spirals like mineral to corn stalk,
water to sedge grass, seed to chicken beak.

Spring wind flips white curtains
out upstairs window.
The chicken scratches, considers
where to lay her egg.

She will not be seduced by
macho rooster into cozy coop.
She has been letting her wings grow.

The willow's long fingers urge,
USE THEM NOW.
Chicken muscles tense, wings lift.
Chicken sails to curtain-haired window,
white as she is.

Cool inside, cool quilt chicken-scratch
where white chicken lays her egg,
necklace fallen into the bed's depression.
This jewel hides evening sun and slough lily.
You could call it a MEMO to John Green,
Mrs. Green: Start here, start anywhere.
Scratch in the dirt, beak to the ground.

The Annunciation

In Leonardo's painting, she studies
out of doors, this eminent virgin
in her habitual cloth of red and blue.

Before her on a pedestal table
encrusted with a mollusk shell, lies
an open book from which she raises her eyes

to the boy dressed in swan's wings, wearing
a cap of curls and carrying a lily wand.
She may have seen him ahead of her

in church, his shoulders and torso
masculine and square, his hair
a tangle of innuendo.

That he comes to her in the garb
of heaven is only an accident
of myth and history, for she needs

nothing announced. The cleft in the palm
of her raised hand anticipates all he means
and she accepts only provisionally,

for he is her inspiration, not a winged
word or an unborn child. This child-man,
with fabulous pinions, will cause her

to abandon the protected corner,
to crush the low, delicate plants
and dream his weight will never rise.

At the Edge Together

Some say we are incompatible—
you air, I earth. At night
I sleep to wake in worry, and you
grind your teeth and still sleep.
Awake, we have different gestures.
Giving up what troubles you,
your palm falls open on the table,
but my fist closes tight to enjoy
a pain. Even empty, our clothes
tell how differently we move. Lined
against a wall, my shoes still trip me,
but your trousers, hung from a door,
never catch the dust, so lightly
do their hems lift from the ground.

One summer when we were divided
by an ocean, I saw you as a thin sail
drawn tight against the wind, and as I waited
at the dock, you appeared, white figure
on a balcony. You leaned on the railing
as below I wondered
what you had left behind
in the dark room
to breathe the harbor air
and why you waited
for my boat to leave.

Gone from you, I saw you everywhere.
Now we walk past places we've known,
a cellar bedroom with one
high-curtained window, a small lake
bordered with redwing nests.
We protect a life neither of us
could make alone. What disaster
can break the hinge that binds us
at the edge together?

Midwestern Epic

A stranger, *forestiere* in Italian,
outsider in Minnesota
on a train through fields raucous with sunflowers,
change to a local, a milk-train
to grandfather's small town Dakota.
My vision double, containing the Italy
of another grandfather I knew only
from strangers gesturing on a station platform,
fingers plucking angry fruit.
My German grandfather met us in a pickup,
chaff stuck in the seat grooves.
My sister so young for her benefit
I ignored cows humping. Prairie horizon
with one wagon high against drowning blue.
Children of the South, we came summers,
now one more time return, the town's shrunk
around a silo, old house cut
into barn-red apartments where on the front porch
petunias burned their midnight scent into my doll carriage,
tea cups. This town's walk has gone into a stroll.
I stand by the convent where a nun
guided my nervous hand through a series of chords.
Gone for years, the piano by her window
returns, strange music
like memory unbidden,
a child against dark spruce.

Chokecherry Summers

In that photograph of North Dakota summer
my mother's skirt fanned a flame
from a bucket of bitter fruit.
I grew every year in its heat,
my sister's mouth
red with plum juice.

One summer I slept
on pantry shelves, under paraffin,
field rabbit escaped from
a baby's cradle, red grief
howled awake, trembling,
caught in a silver ring.

Next summer, imprisoned
in backstairs tower,
I imagined them, mother
and grandfather, plotting
to strangle me like
grandmother lavender,
a strand of her grey hair,
molecules in sunlight
transparent as death,
wrapped on my finger,
cut off the blood.

My mother the daughter,
lighting the stove, making the beds.
The summer I ran three miles to Lake Elsie,
calling my father, absent again.
The hot August morning
blood ran down my legs,
I hated my mother
in her separate white room.
She cut me a patch
from grandfather's shirt.
She didn't tell me

each day I wore him
slowly he'd die.

Next a summer with my father
far from Dakota. His big toe
soaked in Epsom salts. I baited
hooks with bread for him, cut
index-card houses—bed, table
and chairs, wanted to marry him,
but he only played violin
with me at the piano
home from the train.

> Finally a walk to the lake
> past chokecherry, plum.
> I speak to a farmer
> scything a meadow.
> My cousin is king, and I
> am his queen. We rule
> thirst hot as hornets,
> fierce as bloodsucker kisses.
> We turn mother to jelly,
> sister to song, and send grandfather
> to live with a stone.

Dakota Turkey

Fat thighs, blue after a week
on the train. In its mottled
gullet my mother pushed
her arm to the sleeve.
We stood back, afraid of
slippery liver, fist of heart.

Papa Max sent sausages too,
chain links to Dakota,
which didn't explain
this host of winter, barn of a bird.

Our mother already tasted
dark meat, but in our short, green days
we couldn't grasp how cold
that banged its drum on frigid night,
that let silence fatten into final heat,
how breast and wings so cold
could bring her joy.

We wanted her more like the game-hen
southern mothers who daily laid
clucks and kisses, fanned their feathers
and never labored to give off warmth.

We wanted her more lax in our persistent
heat. While she, the northern larder,
stashed words and love against
a season that came just once a year,
brown-parceled, gelid, raw.

Uncle Tonio

1.
My uncle's black chest hair
   lifts bulletproof
           from his undershirt.
Morning now, he sits at my mahogany table
   smoking Winstons.

2.   Last night
circling in from Chicago, this youngest uncle
   rose up dark
           and square on the landing.
My eyes x-rayed through
   fly and underwear
           to the prostate giving him hell.
Female hormones
   make his parts go floppy.
He quipped, "Soon I'll be a cow
   in your china shop."

3. He wants coffee
           stronger than I can make.
Inside the breakfront, china clinks.
   He'll eat a lot.
           I know the hunger of those teeth.
I know the strut of this youngest brother.

4. My father's a pullet
           compared to this cock of the walk
who spun whores into officers' beds
   throughout Naples.
           OSS air-dropped him into the Vatican
where he teased enough amontillado under a prelate's cassock
   to filch secret papers
           for Roosevelt. Champion emissary

with the gutter's argot, he didn't learn this lingo
   from my father
       who traces his lineage from Dante.
Nor from the patriarch their father, though the Papa
   performed great feats,
       followed four professions
and wrote letters home for a thousand countrymen.
   No, this crower descends
       from the strega herself,
Grandma Philomena who dove into the American orb
   but never converted
       to daytime English. Instead
on the backstairs, she built a cabal of four grandsons
   court-martialed from the table.
       She put them to bed,
fed them from her magic apron and schooled them to know
   the evil eye,
       and the moon's countless horsemen.

5.
Some squirmed free. My father made solitary homage
   to collars and parlor piano.
       But Tonio who knew her longest
she blessed with the least shame, the most Italian.

6.
I should have known he wouldn't last, soon would drag
   his weighty tool to bed. As he lay dying,
       couldn't know he'd kid of half-masts or soggy carrots,
   squawk to my father
       like their boyhood crow.
Couldn't have guessed, long after his juice was cooked
   that my father, the elder brother

    would survive into such foolish disorder
he'd hear the clatter of dishes as false teeth dropping.

7.
Now, five years dead, Tonio, you cackle at us—
 how we beg you to keep it quiet
when the whole uproarious load has overturned,
 the songster brays
    like an ass, and I am left
holding a flower no straighter than the noodle
 you said would never again
    come *al dente* to the table.

Between the Houses:

Old Notions

A civil snow stretches its haunches
to greet you on the steps. The porch

offers frosted cheek to clouds
who play at backyard summer laundry.

Strollers crunch their boots
through this icy solstice,

discreet and grey except for
the sky robber who flashes a spectral

continent across the neighbor's
sun room. And the white pine

that stretches its wingtips
to winters when wolves,

red-eyed and starving,
kept you solaced

on the frozen edge of the
wide-shouldered absolute.

Relations

If you wonder why six women
pose in black gowns with some relief
of lace or jewel at the neck,
look at their faces: down-turned mouths,
staring eyes. The mothers behind
have fostered the daughters in front.
Fatherhood forgotten, they perch
at black-bird gravesites.
They ride the unsteady roofs
of houses in flood. Their skirts
shelter fears, dust
driven through walls, settling
a pall on clean linen,
grit in the mouth.

A descendent stoops to wipe
dirt from the floor.
Her baby cries. Vapor fills
rooms with their unmistakable
hands, clenching, relaxing.

They have collected buttons and string,
shards of skirt and apron
until their names are sewn crazy
across fields. I have known
six women to spend
hundreds of stitches
on a quilt that went to warm
a tractor in winter.

To My Mother at 82

You-you-you, there's no one like...
from wiglet to feet crippled
after years in pointy-toed shoes.
Your hikes across town now mince
the steps of a Chinese doll.

You pick the hurricane rose and lament
each limb you hacked and cleared.

You-you, late-night seamstress of rompers
from your husband's trousers.
Now he's dead, you pass his long johns to me.

You-you, with your father, whitewashed
the kitchen over your mother's breakdown.
Now, you never speak of her.

Finally I understand you—truth
in small talk, pretty
arrangements of crushed
bones. You hobble

over our rough road
and for the first time, lean
on my arm, while I, who have dug
into unhealthy ground for the ways
we are, I watch you among

school children as a candlemaker
carves wax to burn deep and cast
over your humped shape and their ripe forms,

a soft light, come full circle

even from the side we cannot see.

Painted Cheeks

Baby doll dressed in lace cap
and ruffled arms, someone
pressed a pouty chin and high cheeks
in your face. Left you
in the attic until
the dog scratched on the stairs.

With wagging tail and back-swept grin
he saved you, dragged from grandma's trunk.

You were supposed to teach girls
the stroller strut, boys
the lemonade swoon.

Over the years your eyes
rolled up in your head,
hair fell off.

For the tiny coffin, they repainted
your cheeks. Grandma couldn't remember
who made you, whose belly
stretched daily over the sink,
whose fingers pushed your hard arms
into their final, lasting sleeves.

Grandmother

Lower your chin, Momma,
relax your eyes.
Let your knife quiver
in the hog's head. Your hands
are big as hams. When the Sioux brave
wanted your scalp, your hair
waved around his arrow,
caught in its tendrilled gold.

You advised the young student,
your grandson, his pet pig
would grow into a hog.
But he curried and oiled,
led the pig to school.
Its pink breath erased
the earth's continents,
planets' names while
snow covered the way home.
Think of them there
in the smoky room, in love
with the shirtwaisted teacher,
slowly forgetting how to spell
Africa, Uranus; how gerunds
end in "g." If they'd floundered
in the Dakota blizzard,
two jujubes in a summer cone,
think of the pleasure your knife
would have lost, lifted, waiting.
Then the slice through air.
Cupboards blanch. The blade
halves a skull. Flesh parts
and all of Pharaoh's army
slides lifeless onto the tin
of your drain board.

Mad history runs pig red
through your fingers.

Math Whiz

The math whiz stands behind his buddies
hamming it up in front of the camera.
His hands tuck under suspenders
as the great hunters cluster in the snow.
One in beret sights a rifle, one
saws a haunch off a frozen stag,
while the white-shirted math whiz
counts buttons and the hairs
on his buddies' necks. Soon
they will go in for grub slung by two angels
washed-out in the center, pale
from light and snow, from turning
their backs on men who stare.

Looking toward the commercial future,
to towns and parquet floors, the math whiz
hangs back, lets others break the spine
of the frontier. Then clinking the broken
vertebrae of lumber, wheat, Dust Bowl
farms into his open till,
he'll build furniture and hardware store,
post office and morgue. He'll put
he-men in his debt, and make all women,
daughters included, his certain accomplices.
Without lifting a finger, he'll tote up
their worth, columns in his head, computing
their lives with his genius for figures.

Missionary

Named for the evangelist, the voice
crying in the wilderness
of America, John the Baptist
Italiano became Protestant,
boomed from his pulpit.
"A great orator," his son,
my father, will repeat,
"a great orator."

Who led the family, wife and four boys,
up the slanting streets of Pittsburgh
into Wop Town, Sunday after Sunday.
From the streetcar stop
they climbed past the raw
houses of Catholics. "Betrayer"
"Heretic" "Dirty Protestant"—
voices pelted; eggs, tomatoes
splattered the sidewalk
and the trousers of the son,
Leonard my father, who wanted
to be clean, who could not
wash his hands enough
before eating, but earned
the name "Egg Face" from his brothers
because he had learned
not to feel the crusted dirty yolk.

Between the Houses:

Soot

What we want to believe
about the way a life
can suddenly look up
and reward us

is stalled and slipping
against a spur
of downspout,

smudged and idled
under adjacent windows.

Eaves work
to shore up
a sulfur sky.
A tree offers
its denuded branches

but the word of the day
is "Pass on," like the
shoulder of
a garage, edging

out of sight
behind the
empty hollow
of a rain barrel.

Orion's Sword

We drive through the long tube of Iowa
through hooded December
into Missouri hills:
Resolve into focus.

You pale as a birch stand almost too tall
for the awkward roof. In the woods
Okies castrate squalling hogs.

At night, sounds stream to us
across the airwaves of America:
Chicago, D.C., Amarillo.

I am reading Malamud,
black and white against
your unresolved color on the bed.

How can I already know
what it will take me years
to express? That I am folded

into the inner pocket
of a jacket you choose
never to wear.

And my part? Years later
I will remember you
as paddler in the stern

while the river
with riffles and foam
tongued against
me in the prow.

In the night sky
Orion wheeled drunkenly,

belt and sword pointing
untold distances on
the way north.

Winter Mood

After a week of snow,
windshield clogged with salt,
the woodpile next door stares with eyes
cut from summer's trees.
It is a time for courage and the slow heart.

On the kitchen table, a jar of basil
reminds me of summer when distance
announced its sweetness through long evenings
and what we did not know entered
the morning mind. Now the only illusion
is your blue-shirted arm reflected
in a window darkened into mirror.

At times we have little to say
or else words fly to leave us cold.
Surely we can blame the season,
but in the quiet, the slow descent
of what may happen
weights us to the ground.

Body Count

Finally, after three bars
we settle in the courtyard at Moody's.
Your brother and sister
and I try to talk
while you ignore me with your eyes.
Sycamores and poplars cut the sky
and in the dark, cigarettes hover.
Your brother who used to catch fireflies
now has snagged your eyes
as he talks of Gary and the mills.

The city of Gary is blasted.
Men drink or lose a hand in the steel
and women who work the mills
turn rough and use the men's convenience.
Skirt above my knees, I rest
a heel on your tilted chair,
your arm warm, I spell there
the word for love.
You settle the chair
and scold my feet away.

Counting the times I speak
and your eyes remain on your brother,
I hear him say how American soldiers
counted women and children dead
to claim a Vietnamese village.
Blasted with drink and disease,
we count down
to the numbers on our graves,
and I play Hangman
with the letters
of our names.

Bridge of Sighs

Above the sofa, Dante gazes at Beatrice while
Grandpa complains of his joints and bowels.
His second wife rolls the roast Italienne.

All the china of their lives is glassed
in this small house under McKeesport soot.
I'm here to sort it out. Grandpa,

I want the truth, not some tale told
by your sons, but virgin truth
in your own tongue, why did you leave?

They say you went down from Pescopagano,
entered a seminary in the city until
cholera took you. You lay in the hospital

until family friends brought you their daughter.
Desire fluttered like wings
trapped in an innocence of sheet.

Now is this right? Or should I trust
the other tale that has you challenge the church
to shout "Viva" for the king. Defrocked,

you crossed the ocean to preach Protestant
and marry a minister's daughter.
Which is it, Grandpa, please, before you die.

* * *

Nothing, you answer nothing. Nothing
in your eyes but their watery clouds.
You give me nothing but another question:

"Can I trust that electric blanket not to burn?"
I've brought it to ease your joints, but nothing
I say will make you use it. Old tightrope walker,

you rise above me: you have a date with the bathroom
throne. And I am left to imagine you
young again. It is evening: sun and moon conjoin

to guide you over rooftops for one last
glimpse of the girl you loved. Hair crackles
from her brush, spins candlelight to gold.

While here, years gone, smoke curls
over new wine, American provolone.
What, then, do they prove, that hair, this smoke?

Our table is wound with sighs. Heads bow down.
Iced tea pools on the red Formica.
And I am left hungering that you will tell me,

as you sit in pain, in your old man's
clothes, as you take beside me the wine
and cheese we both know are neither good nor true.

Between the Houses:

Glacial Eyebrows

Because the sky
behind the normal cornice
and backyard fence

is burning

and no one has noticed
in the stair-step windows

because the front lawn
raises glacial eyebrows,

its stare bold and blind
as a carnival barker's.

And the wires
above the subdued garage
are chopped, midair

by opposing hatchets
of bedroom windows...

If you want to get a message through

don't count on the lighthouse
stalled between the houses.

The sky will simply
burn itself out.

And you, reefing
sails, proceed

with no idea
of where to install

this coffin
of remembered summer.

Gravestones

After I hinted if you wanted
a bigger room, we'd have to move,
you clung to this house—"I'll live here
forever, bury me
in the backyard, if they'll let you,
and I'll tell you, Mom,
what I want on my grave,
put my picture and underneath,
a picture of the cabin and one
of Jessie in her braids."

Lying on the big bed trampoline,
girl with braids of your own,
I have to tell you, I've never
thought of gravestones except
to admire Keats' line, his name
was water. But when you ask,
I imagine granite
covered with an open book.

I am with you, deep in the backyard,
under the onion humus,
under the tent I saw
from the second floor
that summer night you slept
with noisy cats
and a biography
of George Washington.

We lie under each other's hair,
under your grave imaginings,
two photos in the cold backyard.

Walking by the Wall

Strong-legged daughter of ten,
reluctant you went with me
along the river road. What need
had you for exercise?
I was the one, when you
were smaller than one day's cry,
felt I must pull you into being.
Now you weight my arm.
Wooing, I tell you
the golden lilies close at night,
and picking one, you say,
"Daylilies, I know."

Above the freeway,
you run your hand along
the wall, concrete slabs
that alternate rough
and smooth. You call,
"The rough is cooler
than the smooth." It's your game
I play, putting my hands
against the slabs. I don't want
to tell you that the sun,
which glows and sinks behind
the wall, makes neither warmer
to my touch. So faking,
I give a reason. "The rough,
with more ridges, cools.
The smooth keeps the heat it holds."
You walk ahead, drop
the lily and turn
to tell me, "Mother,
you always know,
you never let me wonder."

The Iris Garden

1. Flags on the edge of fast-moving water
or in a vase where light falls across a mantel,
a Black Swan collects the day in its inky folds.

Each spring a cardinal stakes its territory of notes
in naked branches. The garden stitches a garment,
blood pulsing, lips parted. My fingers brush
the red beard of a creamy iris.

2. To domesticate myself first married, I learned
the wildflowers, May apple, trillium, a nub of breast
on a stalk. I puttered in the kitchen, watched trees
weave an openwork against the sky. Then closer-grained
bloomed silk peonies, velvet pansies until the iris
cut a more human figure who made lineage possible.

At the iris garden between rows of Peach Frost and October Ale
my daughter gathered iris falls. Mr. Gable, the gardener,
distracted by orders for Minnesota Skies and Lilac Haze,
let us wander to the back. Along the fence she learned
the first sad fact of flowerhood: piles of dying heads,
petals scratched, colors bleeding into brown. Planted again,
the heads toppled. Her kisses tore their transparent flesh.

3. When she was tall enough to dwarf the iris, Mr. Gable died.
Another spring, I walked out of the marriage, arcs of flowers,
steady fence. Divorce a memory as of death, I grow along with her
except when, tired after a bath, her face small under turbaned
towel, the heavy grace of womanhood weights her slender stalk.
Memory of crushed iris, decorum thinned to gauze,
we have no name for this dying.

4. In a new house, a friend told her husband that the iris
growing from the bricks would match their purple
with a scent of grape. "Iris don't smell," he said.
Cut, the iris splashed their table with a bouquet of wine.
"My father's garden," she said. He kissed her jaw
where a down of hair flushed over the cheek.

First, lovers exchange the gift of their past. Gentle iris,
through your wide pupils light streams down a corridor.
The seeds wait, remembering, dreaming. Light
makes their bodies knowing, and for another spring,
memory rises iridescent from damp ground.

Galleries

Last Midsummer's eve your new growth
wilted in the heat. Air outside
tittered with the crowds.
I thought the art gallery
would quiet you.

There you paused in an alcove,
gazed into the courtyard below.
Against its gentle drop, only a hint,
your elbow sang sharp as high C.
Behind you the paintings glistened
blue against green, mauve
for rain on plowed dirt.
They had designed my world
for years, but what could I call
your spectral growth, unnatural white?

Fourteen years climbed pointed toes,
moonswept hair. Taller than octave,
you vibrated a woman's tremolo. For the first time
I saw your elbow curve a bowl of light
with you in its center. Now in winter,
your bedroom walls crowd more and more
heads of the Beatles. You adore them, blame me
for not knowing them, "I am in mourning
for something I missed by twenty years."

My darling, like you I danced in movie darkness,
sang songs I thought my parents never heard.
They noticed only silence, my body
turned inward until a stranger took my elbow
and broke what I, like you, had been born to lose.

The Chicken

One night in the country of colonels,
a girl dreams her grandmother
chops the head off a chicken.
Open beak in the dust, wings
flecked with blood. The grandmother

grabs the neck and peels down the gullet.
The student steps out, tiny doll
shot from a cannon. Free and livid,
she wants an apricot.

The old woman shakes a fruit at her:
"You should have stayed hidden
through plucking and stewing.
Been served at the table.

Entered the bloodline of your
country." The student tears
at the fruit. Its hard pit scrapes
her throat. Should she squawk a warning?

Will anybody listen?
The grandmother has her eye
to a keyhole. To the room
where the colonels eat chicken.

In the morning feathers drift
the bed, message formed before
her legs sweep it away:
it spells hers, her country's fate:

"The simplest words in the shape
of a key, the smallest person with a hand
for the knob, the choicest rebellion
in the choke of a bone."

The Last Seal in the Baltic

Summer 1988

1.
On the coast of Sweden
seals wash up in singles
and in groups, dead from

a lung disease. They are weakened
by chemicals and sewage
dumped untreated into

their remote, cold sea. An arc
of world away, by another
northern sea, they reappear

as grey, undulating rocks
covered and uncovered
by tea-clear water.

2.
Day after day they die
until by summer's end
all grey seals

compute a soundless
O. Constant water
brings back the loss.

Rapid flippers, clown-fringed eyes,
their nostrils no longer
snap closed to dive.

3.
By August, grey seals balloon
under my ribs. Listen,
hearts drum under lungs

stretched tight for dying,
distance compressed
to a lifetime.

4.
On the coast of Sweden
the heart drum is silent.
I curve my body around

a seal's cold side,
incomplete lover who finds
forgiveness only in the grave.

Listen to the heart drum
here, where I sit at a blue
table by a window.

Water blue through
continents of pulse
to the drum edge of horizon.

Between the Houses:

Summer Sideshow

The fire escape whooshes
into its own tangled
net of surprise
above the parlor greenway.

Under the eaves, two lives
rock and roll
in Grandma's
sleigh bed.

Beyond the bay window,
cutlery has deboned
any number
of exquisite restraints,

and out here
the lightning-bolt driveway
is swept clean

as any carney
man's whistle.

The family car
can still rocket
to earthtime

any summer day.
While against the sky,

roofs—crazy as cracked
mirrors—package their own

convenient

house of horrors.

My Mother's Leaving

Who would have guessed she didn't have everything—
best house in town, lawn courts in back?

Her brother, the tennis twin, still let her win
and once on a dare she outran the freight to the slough.

With her father on back roads, she sat at the wheel
while he buried the dead, bought up farms

for back taxes. With her mother retiring and
her brother thought dull, she was prize Kuchen.

The world's wealth mailed to her, oranges and oysters.

*

Directions said nine months to master the instrument
but she wouldn't practice scales or one-piano duets.

The piano sat there, made the floor sag.
Much later in summers, her own child banged chords.

By then she was canning red jelly in jars.
Her mother had died. She was queen of the realm.

Hot nights on the porch, her hair tugged the elms.
If she had any sorrow, only doves heard.

Brisk single walker, she was often alone,
except once, still early, her daughter yanked after her.

When church bells stopped ringing, she was beating the girl.
Whatever had caused it, she was simply too proud,

couldn't stand her child's antics, up with the birds,
wouldn't take castoffs from the sister-in-law's girls.

The family was hers, and she couldn't bear sharing.
From the moment she left, her father condemned her,

let the sister-in-law feed him. Gave her name to a bird.

*

Afterwards, did she ever come back? Wet the walk with her
tears? Once after rain, she paused by the Hardware,

gold H in her hair. By then her brother owned everything.
She had built a house far away. She could have used

a fridge or a stove, but he offered a disposal.
She had it put in. Who knows if it worked?

Remember things broke when they were first made?
This one was worth just what it cost her: nothing,

disposed of. No one saw her afterwards.

Mudpies

I, the bully mom, pose outside the packing crate,
home owner, ready to move on, but defending the price.

Inside, my sister hunches on a Mexican chair, mixes
leaves with mud. She won't look up. Housebreaker

Bobby Moon, in cowboy hat, spins his six-shooter at me.
In half a sec, he'll overturn the little table, spill the juice,

grind mudpies into the floor. He will not repent
until I scoop down my pants under the oleander bush

and show him the cream of my pee. Such penalties of housekeeping
I've learned early from the half-light where my father

lassos his voice around my mother's legs. She stands
at the sink. Her slip shows. He'll criticize

the meatloaf next, then her pressing job. He'll corral her
until, to tame him, she sponges his shirt, hitches her slip,

loads on the pepper until she rules the door
with cold fatigue, ready to extract her due

when I cross the threshold. In the frozen cream
of her love, my plastic spoon sinks and snaps, leaving her

the round and carrying part of me, while I hold
a makeshift sword that scratches every time I try to feed myself.

Southern Combustion 1959

It started slowly as I sat against the chintz
and cabbage roses of my mother's living room.
The sun lowered a notch and struck
the brass buckle of my father's belt
dead center. He wobbled from his chair,
dripping with heat. On TV a black man
had kissed a white woman. I tried telling
him I was innocent. No black boy would ever
speak to me. All I wanted was to be white
and pretty.

My doll's voice withered in his heat.
Pretty soon, a black stud would knock
at our door, he thundered, and I, his older
daughter, would have to answer it.
What happened next ignited the curtains.
Cabbage roses swam across his face.
Scatter rugs, my glasses, Dale Carnegie's
How to Win Friends and Influence People
loosened in the rush and swamped us both.
Huge black lips in my father's face
rose over the land, pressed over
my eyes, cut off breath.

We went under. Sputtering,
I grasped anything solid:
table, piano leg, the family Bible.
The Lord had promised against floods.
From this scant text I forced back tides,
and sassed the wind. Curtains settled,
cabbage roses clustered the walls.
My father, soaked and spent,
sat dripping in a pool of lamplight.

Tiptoeing close, I set the paper before him.
When next he peeked at me, I was again
his pet daughter, playing safe

from the petting and kissing that soon
would start, his good girl, obedient,
checking her mascara in a tiny mirror.

Her Letter to a Patron

Naples 1649

from the painter Artemisia Gentileschi

Since you ask the price
of my figures, I will tell you,
Senor: one hundred scudi per figure
or you will not possess
a canvas by Artemisia.
My painted flesh will never crack
like Anguissoula's. She clothed
herself in reticent colors.
My Judith's strong arm
ends in a sword.

In each canvas I battle
with light and shade, so
at nineteen, I was taught
by the man my father hired.
His hand guided mine
as we painted callas,
their red heads hissing
with sun. We entered the clash
of ash and flame until
as I commanded surrender,
he broke the brush
from my hand, tore
the clothes from my breast,
and forced me to the ground.
Thumbscrew at my nail,
I was accused of inviting rape,
but I defended only my virtue
lost in a fallen brush.

Now I paint Judith.
Unarmed, she walked
into the tent of Holofernes.
With only a candle,

she made him drunk
with ease and certainty.

My maid holds the fruit
of the general's head
while I, with sword
and candle, listen
for the approach of fame.
You ask for a madonna.
Senor, my madonnas are few.
Mary means nothing to me.
I have beheaded many men.

Florence Nightingale Receives a Visitor

> Don't ask me if I remember
> your father. I cut the blood-soaked
> cloth from his legs. After the Battle
> of Inkerman, men lay in their own filth.
> I ordered scrubbing brushes and beds.

The minarets of Mihrimah Cami mosque
rise outside the second-floor window.
I coil ropes of linen. At night
a nurse falls in her own stupor,
skirts stain a punctured chest.
She is removed to England.

> For thirty years I've lain here,
> letters and viceroys pass the straits.
> Your father lived with a lost leg.

Under the dome of Hagia Sophia
a cat stalks, its eyes wide
as the wake eyes of wounded
in pain. Divine wisdom
brought me here, out of whaleboned
convention, to treat an army.
Each crusted face and open wound,
I bathe and wrap.
Distant and sharp, a bell rings,
pebble slaps the surface.
I fall through clean water to rest,
my head to the East.

> Don't think I cannot see you.
> Like your father, you want me
> to fall in your eyes. Young man,
> I am already drowned. I snubbed
> Lord Herbert before he died.

Between the Houses:

March Thaw

When sorrow stokes walls
with disappearing beds,

> Chant blue hats, blue shadows.

When cold veers its sheets
into frozen monuments,

> Eye charcoal chimney,
> that warm pole.

Don't expect to nestle
against a bolster of fence.

Or slap silly in a suck
of mud. Winter's blanket

Has been yanked, and all
its furniture, shocked,

Raw, leers haphazard
against the open studs.

After Dachau

Note it down in the accounts,
I spent too much for wine tonight.
I sat in a fine Italian restaurant
on a quiet residential street
in Munich and drank a half liter
of Trevino di Arezzo,
to wash away the bungholes
with no flesh around them,
the jiggling bodies in wagons
local farmers buried
in their fields.

I did not cry at Dachau,
in the documentary studio (only
250 allowed...we would understand,
for safety reasons), though
tears stung at the moment
of liberation, when pans
were shaken carefully over
fire, a stick arranging beans
like flowers on a grave,
ritually placed. (I thought about
bringing flowers, but did not.
Two gardeners planted begonias
around the crematorium,
at various enclaves: Rifle Range,
Ashes Stored Here, Grave
of a Thousand Unknown.)

I drank four-plus glasses
of Trevino di Arezzo (and remembered
I know an American woman who has moved
to Arezzo. She grows iris.
The young Italian who loves her
picks her flowers when
she has lost her voice.

Flowers are for when
we cannot speak).

With the wine
I ate a salad and penne noodles,
in garlic/basil/tomato sauce.
I told the signora it was *squisito*.
All this, while deep-set eyes
and sunken ribs floated
over the white porcelain plate
of red penne (for wings),
and I drained the squat bottle
(mezzo litre) dry.

What can I
or anyone say
about such suffering?
It is a life's work
to survive out of it.

Would I have reacted
like the good citizens (what is
the German word for citizen?)
who covered their mouths
when finally they saw
the mounds of bodies?
Some of us believe
what is good for us,
like this wine,
and do not probe further.

Then, too tired, or sick,
too ignorant to stuff the truth
in our gorge any further, we stand
in the doorway and witness the
harvest, spilled like grain against
the far wall, higher against the wall

and falling in smaller amounts to the
floor, closer to us, arms and legs,
attached to the dumbbells of bodies,
to the helmets of heads, and the boats
of feet with their strings of barnacles.
Sometimes an expression in a face
of such laughter that we expect
the man to lift up from the wall
and give us the joke.

But he does not.
And that is why I,
and so many other
good citizens,
have swallowed
countless bottles
of dry white wine,
in hopes we'll stop waiting
for his voice to tell us
how to live after this,
how to live with the time
it has taken us
to come and see.

The White Room

l. My mother takes pride: she is always practical.
    Whatever is repeated is practical.
    What is washable is practical.
    Whatever is absorbed is practical.

2. Over long-distance, her voice rises and falls. My mother has the life of an ocean. She tells me, "When I brought you home from the hospital, we had just moved. I located the apartment by phone from my bed. If you gave me a phone, there wasn't anything I couldn't do. I hired a practical nurse. She kept you in one room. She fed and changed you. Even though I had a new baby, I unpacked all the boxes."

3. Later, it occurs to me that possibly for less money my mother could have hired someone to unpack the boxes.

4. Still later, I wonder, where was my father?

5. Then a strong memory recurs: my mother stands at the sink. She has her back to me. I talk to her back.

6. Now I imagine that I know the room where the practical nurse kept me. It is immensely white. Its corners dissolve: on the ceiling hovers an unstable mirage. I try to orient myself to a window or door, but the room has no features. It is white light where I swim, passive, aimless, dumb.

7. Eventually we move to a town. It is called Bridgewater. Sick with measles, I float in the half-dark. But this time, the wall has found a window. Light from a florist's sign outside pulses
    red, dark   red, dark.
I follow its rhythm. It matches mine
    red, dark   window, word,   hand, heart.

8. Now that I recognize its origin, I wonder if I should tell my mother about the white room. It has been between us for years. I have never spoken its silence to her. She has been busy as long as I can remember.

9. My mother has the life of an ocean. If I tell her, she
may say, "I had to wash everything by hand and keep you clean.
I didn't have time to sit and hold you."

10. Over the years, I have learned to turn my back to her. I no longer
wait for her to face me.

11. But I want to show her my rhythm
    red, dark   window, word   hand, heart.

12. Maybe someday I will slip my rhythm into her ocean.
Perhaps this is foolish, foredoomed. But if I am careful, if I wait for
unseasonable calm, if I row out far enough, away from the
splashing waves that pound the shore, if I am patient,
let the seventh, highest wave pass, then ask her to come,
she might brush my cheek with spray, she might rock me.
She might slosh herself into the boat, under my feet,
and all the way home, nurse my toes with little nibbles.

13. Perhaps I owe her this. Someday soon, the white room may absorb
her. They both are practical. Perhaps I should warn her before it is
too late.

14. But I am afraid of her. If she comes too close, she may overpower
me and I may drown. To begin, I must trust us both.

15. Time urges me to show her my play. Can I float in her ocean,
remembered, unwashed, unique, impractical? Can the ocean calm its
rush long enough to learn a rocking song?

To the Funeral and After

1. In the long box he lay
like a violin, hands
clasped more prim
than life, the ring absent.
   Head shrunken
   into nobility.
   The once tan skin
   gone pale, the hair
   thin and subdued
   to the scalp.

While the preacher pumped my grief,
I glimpsed, rising above the coffin rim,
his nostrils broad as life,
wide as the moon,
and vulgar with hair.
They were the only sign I had
that his flesh still held.

We buried him in a steel box
in red clay by the Cooper River.
In the distance, the bridge
draped its steel lace
over his former maniac desires.

2. North and home, my grief
turned in the lathe of fall.
A coffin of air took shape,
but he would not
lie down. The man
once my father
was nowhere to be found.

I went on like this, sorrow
aching to be set in ground
as air cooled, and the school bus
took the children away.

3. After first frost, I walked out
to the zinnias that still flaunted
red and yellow above their
crumpled leaves. Petals
crisp between my fingers
gave off a rough tang,
so sure of themselves
they insisted on life

even as my father
   called for onions
     clanged his belt to the floor,
       slipped to a full snore.

Only life so sure of itself
could give off this rough leaving.

4. As I looked down, his nostrils
poked from the dirt.
The ground here swarmed
with hairs and smells of laughter.
The loam scratched, dense
with cold and the fury of teeth.

He lay in the garden of my sorrow
as sure as he had lived,
warm as his hand to slap
or lift a tune.
I had had him once.

5. As he goes, heat lowers
   along my spine
   appetite breaks
   in the crush of leaves.

   My teeth gnaw
   at the roof line.

Late Song

for my mother

She's breaking my heart
after years of glazing and firing.
"My pretty one. You're my pretty one."

Old lady of trembly lips and thin hair—
"My baby. You're my baby."

Her stubbly chin rubs mine.
We kiss good-bye.

"How far away? How far?"
She points to the wheeling birds.
"I tell the birdies you'll come back."

In these last days, there is
no real life apart.

The broken
heart knows
its spill
of joy.

Between the Houses:

Glad Hand

When hostility older than you or I
has tightened the chain-link fence

and manicured shadows to
nervous yawns,

when downspouts angle
all life's venom

onto one bush, and even
pink walls become a slap

in the face, then it's time
for the common touch,

a glad hand of white-hot
shingles, beckoning wing

of neighbor's garage
roof. Time to hike

further for a
neighborly confab

with shop-
cleaning clouds.

Translate

   1.
We played like children,
       scales on the keyboard
practicing Italian,
       subjunctives and dreams,
missing the flats,
       F sharp in G major,
the difficult plurals
       da capo, staccato.
You told about failure,
       long legs on the pedals,
you spoke in Italian,
       long hair down your back.

       2.
       I have lived without husband,
marito, marito
       who married again,
sposato, espoused
       a woman he knew
prima, prima
       he began making a garden
giardino, unsown.
       I have painted the walls,
muri, muri
       I have painted the walls,
grigio, grey.

   3.
Last night we talked
without looking down,
your blue eyes sharp,
you played all the notes,
you spoke in our language,
you said it in English,
       I learn to be single.

    4.
         Not lost in the courtyard,
perdito, perso,
              chasing the sky,
cielo, cielo
              tramps in the garden,
giardino, giardino
              with outstretched hands
mano, mani.
              No longer the girl,
stumbling, running,
              who could never be good,
buona, bene
              followed by tramps
with pockets bulging
              followed by tramps
with misplayed scales.

  5.
No! I hear you
in the language itself
pull the egg
from the snake's mouth,
pull words from the son,
frame daughter's slammed door.
I hear you, amica,
understand all the notes,
speak in our key.

The Scarf

It has come to me now,
the scarf from around
his violin. The blunt
fingers gone, the crooked
elbow gone, the chin
below long sensuous lips
and the shrug of
instrument into shoulder—
that too—and the small
curved woman held out
straight without hands—
gone in the whoosh of death,
a flick of the cape,
presto! the life
sawed off, plunk!
A board dropped, edges raw.

Then, in floats
the scarf, silky and
fluid, tinted with
the turquoise of redheads,
a wash of cream
at its throat, crushed
from years in a case,
on sofas, in back rooms.

He flips the locks,
ripples back the scarf,
reaches in to lift
the glossy body out.

After each birth,
the instrument cries to tune,
rough squawks at the throat,
bow strikes an exclamation.

We take our places—

he under the lamplight,
I at the piano, then
the quivering notes
lay their breath
on my cheek,
draw us through
a dark sleeve of memory.

Thus set free, we lift,
two winged notes,
to beamed and shadowed
ceiling, where we light
together above
the audience who thinks
we come from nowhere
and go back there
but do not know
the miracle of a scarf,
the legerdemain of love.

Evening Drive: Consolation

Now after drought, I whisper
let it be enough that black fields
glisten with rain, and corn
sprigs small shadows down the rows.
Pines, brown but surviving,
light tall candles of new growth.

At this speed, let me harm no one,
as I return from dinner where
my daughter did not speak of animals
tortured for science or abused for meat.
We ate instead tomatoes scented with danger
and mushrooms blond and forgiving
and bread that knew its place.

Alone in this capsule of metal, I accept
a duty to twilight and the gathered
elders of trees. Hands tight
on the wheel I watch for gophers,
knowing only luck can keep them
from my wheels and the memory
of one, head smashed,
legs kept running.

I pass a woodpecker, rare red head
with barred wings, hit on the road.
Sorrow for its body wrapped
in a cloak, its head a blaze of solitude.
Sorrow also for the daughter
who allows no praise of her beauty,
no man to paint her for pleasure.
She too may be wrapped in herself
knocked aside by speed that lets
no other cross, nor anyone join the way.

Tonight, may good passage home
foretell good company for her

in her own good time, as I return
another race survived
through this still and greening land.

No More Back of the Bus

—Charleston, S.C., 1957

If I jumped up, offered
my seat, the old black woman
might be tempted.
But seeing is dangerous,
sitting is illegal.

And she has learned a shuffle
   slower
      than any hate

to carry her up the steps
of a white house,
to the third floor and a room
flounced with ruffles. There
my girlfriend paints her nails
while the old black woman
offers her lunch from
hands cracked and grey

that grip the seat in front of me.

All the meanness of my race
is stuffed in her shopping bags.

She passes on and sits in the back.
The angel of death stares from her eyes.

If I could break the tension
   leap up
      lead her to the front,
         if we could sit opposite

No longer be part of
the meanest show on earth

Just to sit opposite and notice
threads on her handbag, gold

rubbed from its catch,
let my eyes slide comfortably
over her coat,
when we are no more
than two riders, brown
and white, young and old,
two riders in the big front window,
calm in the promise of water and sky
crossing a river to home.

The Ground Carries Us

When blame falls away like a heavy cloak,
we return to the rooftops of moments,
a spire of evergreen that points north,
neighboring cornice of familiar joy. Saturated
with the wash of ecstasy, regret, the sky
must know us from this high window. In loss,
we have turned our faces to stream distracted
into blue. No other champion so sure
as the garage peak, no other grace
so prolonged as apple blossoms in the dusk
beyond the littered table. Jays bugle us
from the stupor of accounts to our better selves.
Here we return when truths are wrung from us.
Our stories have seeped into the soil and
flourish back at us in the distinct
and honored vessels of their forms. To know ourselves
in these companions of place, to carry on
the slow mosaic of rebirth, when
out of damp voices and stolen color,
we fashion identities who can drop
their cloaks at last and array the ground
with patterns that cleanse and harbor
as they are walked upon.

CELLINI'S FORGE

for Paula and Cy DeCosse

Upstream under San Niccolo
downstream under the Vecchio
the Arno twines and flows.

I stand between, maker,
stranger, brought to bliss
by the tumbling falls. Jove descends

in a shower of gold, ravishing
birth for the slayer's hand.
Rays that strike in this smithy of

air shawl and writhe a serpent's
hair, framing a head, a deadly
face until Perseus' sword

cuts Medusa clean and both figures
return to the tumbling green.
Left transfixed, remaining here,

this garland of verse, blinded by
light, chased in the falls,
wreathes an homage in river hair.

Walking the Labyrinth at Villa Maria

(on the Mississippi outside Red Wing, Minnesota)

for Joyce Lyon

The air stands away from us,
crisp and sharp as a hull.
From across the river,
bluffs, seared by drought,
huff the air back at us.

    Step toward the center, turn,
    one behind the other.

Friendship older than half
our lives widens to
contemplation. The deer,
frightened by our presence, now
return to graze the apples.

Lightning burned half this place
one late March storm, grabbed
old wood in a charred embrace.

    Our steps approach,
    riding the whorls.

Losses stream from us, sometimes
reappearing as bands of steel
at the horizon.

    My friend approaches,
    carrying a blossom
    in her face.

The center, glimpsed from every crossing,
gathers us. The sky has leached heat
to cream. Crows pluck themselves
from fields to settle in
family clusters.

At the center, a new tree,
green ash like the cross,
rises from some
unseen source,
water or hope.

MARGOT FORTUNATO GALT grew up in South Carolina but has lived in Minnesota longer than anywhere else. With a PhD in American Studies from the University of Minnesota, she teaches in the graduate school at Hamline University, St. Paul. Her writing includes art criticism, an oral history memoir of Ojibway artist George Morrison (*Turning the Feather Around: My Life in Art*, 1998), books for young readers on women's baseball and Vietnam war resistance, and *The Story in History: Writing Your Way into the American Experience* (1992). A chapbook of poetry, *The Country's Way with Rain*, was published by Kutenai Press, 1994. She has received writing grants and awards from The Loft, the Minnesota State Arts Board, the Jerome Foundation, the Center for Arts Criticism, the Minnesota Humanities Commission, and the Minnesota Historical Society. The series of poems, "Between the Houses," was inspired by Minneapolis artist Delor Erickson's paintings. Residencies at Norcroft, Ragdale, The Anderson Center, and the Dorset Colony have provided valuable writing time, for which she is grateful. She lives in St. Paul with her husband and cats. Their children have flown.

DELOR ERICKSON graduated from Edison High School in Minneapolis and went to art school in Los Angeles. Further study in studio arts at the University of Minnesota gave him "a more expansive notion of what painting could be." Longtime freelance illustrator, he has shown his paintings in Symphony Gallery, White Oak Gallery, at the University of St. Thomas, the American Swedish Institute, and the Granary Gallery in Martha's Vineyard. "While riding a bus a few years ago," he notes, "I saw that the spaces between the houses in Minneapolis were more interesting than the houses themselves. Thus the origin of the series of small paintings which I call Interstices."

LAUREL POETRY COLLECTIVE

A gathering of twenty-three poets and graphic artists living in the Twin Cities area, the Laurel Poetry Collective is a collaboration dedicated to publishing beautiful and affordable books, chapbooks, and broadsides. Started in 2002, its four-year charter is to publish and celebrate, one by one, a book or chapbook by each of its twenty-one poet members. The Laurel members are: Lisa Ann Berg, Teresa Boyer, Annie Breitenbucher, Margot Fortunato Galt, Georgia A. Greeley, Ann Iverson, Mary L. Junge, Deborah Keenan, Joyce Kennedy, Ilze Kļaviņa Mueller, Yvette Nelson, Eileen O'Toole, Kathy Alma Peterson, Regula Russelle, Sylvia Ruud, Tom Ruud, Su Smallen, Susanna Styve, Suzanne Swanson, Nancy M. Walden, Lois Welshons, Pam Wynn, Nolan Zavoral.

For current information about the series—including broadsides, subscriptions, and single copy purchase—visit:

www.laurelpoetry.com

or write:

Laurel Poetry Collective
1168 Laurel Avenue
St. Paul, MN 55104